South Dakota Native Americans

A Kid's Look at Our State's Chiefs, Tribes, Reservations, Powwows, Lore, and More From The Past and the Present

By Carole Marsh

Native American Heritage™

Graphic Design: Lynette Rowe • Cover Design: Victoria DeJoy

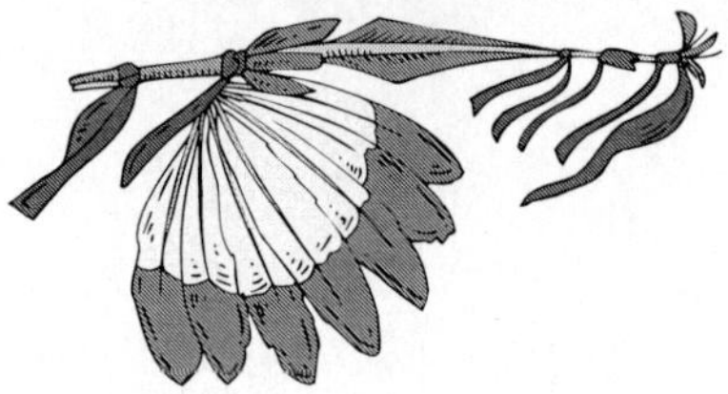

Published by
GALLOPADE™ INTERNATIONAL
800-536-2GET
www.gallopade.com

Gallopade is proud to be a member of these educational organizations and associations:

The National School Supply and Equipment Association (NSSEA)
American Booksellers Association (ABA)
Virginia Educational Media Association (VEMA)
Association of Partners for Public Lands (APPL)
Museum Store Association (MSA)
National Association for Gifted Children (NAGC)
Publishers Marketing Association (PMA)
International Reading Association (IRA)
Association of African American Museums (AAAM)

Native American Heritage™ Series

Native American Big Activity Book

Native American Biographies

Native American Coloring Book

Native American Heritage Book

Native American Timeline

South Dakota State Stuff™

- My First Pocket Guide: South Dakota
- My First Book About South Dakota
- South Dakota Coloring Book
- The Big South Dakota Reproducible Activity Book
- Jeopardy: Answers & Questions About Our State
- South Dakota "Jography!": A Fun Run Through Our State
- South Dakota Gamebooks
- South Dakota Bingo Games
- South Dakota Illustrated Timelines
- South Dakota Project Books
- South Dakota Bulletin Board Set
- South Dakota PosterMap
- South Dakota Stickers
- Let's Discover South Dakota! CD-ROM

Word from the Author

Hello!

I hope you are as interested in North America's wonderful Indian heritage as I am!

Like most kids, I grew up thinking of Indians as the other half of Cowboys. Today, of course, we are getting a much clearer and more accurate picture of what the first peoples on our land were all about. These "facts" are much more fascinating than anything Hollywood can make up. And you probably won't find much of this information in your history textbook!

I am 1/16 Cherokee. This is something I am very proud of and happy about. My grandmother was 1/4 Cherokee. She had tan skin, long gray hair and a very Indian look – especially if I did something bad! Her maiden name was Carrie Corn. Of course, when she got married, she took her husband's name, so it was many years before I learned to appreciate the significance of my native heritage.

Today, I'm trying to make up for lost time by exploring my roots as deeply as I can. One of the most interesting things I've learned is how fascinating all of the Indian tribes are – in the past, the present and future!

As you read about "your" Indians, remember that all native peoples were part of an ever-changing network of time, ideas, power and luck — good and bad. This is certainly a history that is not "dead," but continues to change – often right outside our own back doors! – all the time.

Carole Marsh
She-Who-Writes

PS: Many references show different spellings for the same word. I have tried to select the most common spelling for the time period described. I would not want to be in an Indian spelling bee!

A is for . . .

American Horse

Oglala Sioux chief who persuaded his tribe to sign a treaty which reduced their reservation by half.

Awl

An Indian's "needle." Often made from wood, thorns, bone, or metal, it was used to punch holes in skins so they could be sewn together.

Adze

An Indian woodworking tool used to cut, scrape, or gouge; often used to hollow dugout canoes. Blades were made of stone, shell, bone or copper.

Arikara

Indian tribe that moved to our area around 1400. Also called Arikaree or Ree. Settled on the Missouri River near the South Dakota border. Villagers who hunted and farmed, growing nine types of corn!

Antelope

Used for moccasin tops, pillow stuffing and pipes by South Dakota Indians who also used the animal for food.

Altar

A platform made of rocks or animal skulls; some had bowls, feathers, rattles, or skins on them. Indians prayed at these altars for things like good crops or expert hunting skills.

Arrow

A long, slender shaft made of reed, cane, or wood; pointed tip was attached to one end and split feathers to the other. Feathers helped the arrows fly straight.

Art

The Pawnee and Omaha Indians developed some of the most sophisticated poetry, songs and religious ceremonies of all the Indians of the Great Plains.

Aborigine

A member of the earliest known population of a region.

Arrowhead

The pointed tip of an arrow, made of bone, antler, wood, or iron. Some tips had barbs that would embed themselves in flesh. These barbs made it difficult for an enemy to remove the arrowhead from a wound.

B is for . . .

Big Foot

Miniconjou Sioux chief, and at one time an advocate of the Ghost Dance religion. While leading his people to the Pine Ridge Indian Reservation for refuge, his band was intercepted by the Army and escorted to Wounded Knee Creek. After the Indians set up camp, the soldiers tried to disarm them. The deaf Indian Black Coyote was the only one to resist, which resulted in the Massacre at Wounded Knee. Big Foot and at least 150 of his band were killed.

Band

A subdivision of an Indian tribe. In earlier times, a band was sometimes created when part of a tribe split off from the main group. The band also chose new leadership.

Buffalo

Made up the major diet of many South Dakota Indian tribes. Hides were used as blankets or tents. Every tribe member was given a piece of the animal to eat. There were strict rules about not hunting buffalo alone, so that one person wouldn't scare them all away! To catch the animals, the hunters chased them off cliffs or encircled them in fire, then shot them. A group of 27 tribes is trying to re-establish herds on Indian lands to promote economic development, Indian culture, ecological restoration and spiritual revitalization.

Buckskin

Softened, smoke-treated rawhide. Used by South Dakota Indians to make clothes, bags and pouches.

Battle of Slim Buttes

Just one example of the many skirmishes between whites and Indians who fought over keeping the Black Hills sacred land or mining it for gold. Though the Indians fought to protect this area, they lost out to the intense determination of the whites seeking fortunes.

Bone

Animal bones were used by South Dakota Indians to make buttons, whistles and other items.

Black Hills

Sacred area to the Cheyenne and Sioux. The discovery of gold here led to broken treaties by the whites and retaliation by the Indians. Although the Indians won many battles, they eventually lost the war and were forced to surrender to white ways and live on reservations.

C is for . . .

Cheyenne

Famous Plains Indian tribe that migrated to South Dakota from Minnesota. They lived in villages and farmed until acquiring the horse in the late 1700s. Pushed south out of the Dakotas by the Sioux.

Chief

Leader of a tribe. Different titles meant different things. Some members were made chief because they owned deeds to land. Chieftainship was often inherited, usually from the mother!

Contact Period

What historians call the era in the 1500s when Native Americans first met Europeans. This meeting changed the lifestyle of the South Dakota Indians more than anyone could ever have anticipated!

Crazy Horse Memorial

Requested by Lakota chiefs to be carved in the sacred Black Hills of South Dakota. Located at Thunderhead Mountain Crazy Horse, South Dakota. The site was chosen by Chief Standing Bear and sculptor Korczak Ziolkowski in 1946. The memorial, to be carved in the round, was dedicated on June 3, 1948 with the first blasting. It is a continuing project, and when finished it will show Crazy Horse astride his pony, with his left arm pointing to the lands of his people. The whole project is paid for only with donations. The finished face was dedicated in 1998. When complete, the entire carving will be 641 feet long and 563 feet high—the largest statue in the world! All of nearby Mt. Rushmore would fit into the sculpture's face alone.

Confederacy

A union of different groups of people. A confederacy in Indian culture was a group of tribes that agreed not to fight with each other. They agreed to live peacefully. Sometimes the tribes shared culture and language.

Clan

A tribal unit. Members are descended from the same ancestor.

Citizenship

The Indian Citizenship Act of 1924 states all Indians born in the United States are citizens of the United States, and citizens of the states they live in, even though they may live on a reservation. They can vote. They pay most local, state and federal taxes, including sales taxes.

Crazy Horse

Oglala-Brulé Sioux chief who joined Sitting Bull on the warpath in the early 1870s to resist white gold miners flocking into the Black Hills. In 1876, led his men to victory against General Custer at the battle of Little Big Horn. Eventually surrendered with 800 followers in 1877. He was later arrested, and resisting imprisonment, he was killed.

Calumet

Also called "peace pipe" or "war pipe." Refers to the stem of the pipe, which is decorated with feathers or carved to signal the tribe's intentions. South Dakota Indians believed the calumet to have great power.

D is for . . .

Dance

There were Indian dances for every occasion: war, peace, hunting, rain, good harvests, etc. Drums, rattles, and flutes of bone or reed provided the music. Dancers often chanted or sang while performing. Steps were not easy to learn and required consistent practice.

Dakota

The native name for the Santee branch of the Sioux Indians. The Sioux are the tribe most represented in art as "the" American Indian, usually shown in full eagle headdress, fringed shirt and beaded moccasins. The profile of a Dakota appears on the U.S. penny and nickel. Gave us the word tipi, the red peace pipe, buffalo robes and decorated war ponies. Appeared in Buffalo Bill's Wild West Show. Excellent fighters. Name means "allies," "adders," or "enemies." Around 25,000 Sioux lived in the area during the 17th century.

Descendants

The first South Dakota Indians were descendants of primitive hunters who crossed the Bering Strait from Asia to what is now Alaska. At that time, glacial ice still covered most of North America. These people were the true discoverers of the "New World!"

Disease

South Dakota Indians had no immunity to the diseases that white explorers, colonists and settlers brought to their lands. These diseases included smallpox, measles, tuberculosis and others, which ravaged the tribes in great epidemics that killed many, and sometimes all, members of a tribe.

Deloria, Vine Jr.

Born in Martin, South Dakota in 1933. A famous Yankton Sioux author and teacher, writing often about Indians and the federal government. At one time he was the executive director of the National Congress of American Indians. One of his most notable books is *Custer Died for Your Sins: An Indian Manifesto*.

Dishes

Made from clay, bark, wood, stone, and other materials, depending on what was available and what food they would be used for.

Dyes

Made of lichens, berries, roots, bark, plants, and other natural materials by Indians in South Dakota. Different colors were used depending on what materials were available and what objects were to be dyed.

Dreams

Important in the Indian tradition. It was believed that dreams were the "windows" to the soul. Many thought a person's hidden desires were expressed in dreams.

E is for . . .

Eagle

An animal used in many Indian ceremonies. Eagle feathers attached to war bonnets and shields communicated an Indian's rank in his tribe and what kinds of deeds he had done. Feathers also adorned rattles, pipes, baskets, and prayer sticks.

Even Today!

These Indian reservations are located in South Dakota today: Cheyenne River Reservation, home to Mnicoujou, Itazipco, Sihasapa and Oohenumpa Lakota Sioux bands on 1,419,504 acres ; Crow Creek Reservation, home to Mdewakanton Santee and Ihanktonwan (Yankton) bands on 122,531 acres; Flandreau Santee Sioux Reservation, home to Mdewakanton, Wahpeton, Wahpekute, and Sisseton Santee bands on 2,356 acres; Lake Traverse Reservation, home to Sisseton and Wahpeton Santee Sioux bands on 107,245 acres; Lower Brule Reservation, home to Kul Wicasa Oyate Brulé Teton on 240,000 acres; Pine Ridge Reservation, home to Oglala Lakota Sioux on 1,771,082 acres; Rosebud Reservation, home to Sicangu Lakota Oyate on 954, 571 acres; Standing Rock Reservation, home to Yanktonai, Hunkpapa, and Blackfoot Sioux bands on 847,799 acres; Yankton Reservation, home to Yankton, Yanktonai, and Assiniboine Sioux bands on 434,932 acres.

Earrings

Medicine men sometimes pierced male and female ears at special ceremonies. Earrings, which cost parents or relatives a significant amount, symbolized wealth and distinction. The more earrings that an Indian wore, the greater his honor. Some earrings measured 12 inches in length!

Everyone Should Visit!:

These outstanding South Dakota Indian sites: Akta Lakota Museum at St. Joseph's Indian School, Chamberlain; Buechel Memorial Lakota Museum at St. Francis Indian Mission, Saint Francis; Friends of the Middle Border Museum of American Indian and Pioneer Life, Mitchell; H.V.J. Lakota Cultural Center at the Cheyenne River Reservation, Eagle Butte; The Heritage Center at the Red Cloud Indian School, Pine Ridge; Indian Museum of North America, Crazy Horse; The Journey Museum (includes the Sioux Indian Museum), Rapid City; Klein Museum, Mobridge; The Museum of the South Dakota State Historical Society, Pierre; Oscar Howe Art Center, Mitchell; South Dakota Art Museum, Brookings; Tekakwitha Fine Arts Center, Sisseton; W.H. Over Museum, Vermillion.

Epidemics

Few Indians possessed immunity to the deadly diseases, like smallpox and measles, which European explorers and settlers brought to the New World. As a result, great population loss took place. Sometimes entire tribes became extinct. Epidemics sparked by Hernando De Soto's expedition are estimated to have killed 75% of the native population in the New World.

F is for . . .

Fetish

These small objects were thought to hold the spirit of an animal or a part of nature. A fetish could be an object found in nature, such as bone or wood, or it could be a carved object. The fetish was usually small enough to be carried in a small bag or on a cord. The making and use of a fetish was kept secret by its owner and only shared with the one who inherited it.

Firesteel Creek

Archaeological site of a fortified village of 80 lodges; around 500 – 1,000 people may have lived here about 1,000 years ago. A museum in with artifacts and a replica earthlodge from the site is in Mitchell.

Famous Quote

"Why would you wish to shorten my life by taking my shadow from me?" Oglala Sioux Crazy Horse, refusing to have his picture taken.

Fire Drill

A device used by Indians to make fires which consisted of a stick and a piece of wood with a tight hole in it. The stick was twirled rapidly in the hole, creating friction that would ignite shredded grass or wood powder placed nearby to start a fire.

Farmers

Many South Dakota Indians, ancient and modern, have farming ways! Even pre-contact Indians tilled and irrigated, raising many important crops. Corn, cotton, beans, squash, melons, sunflowers, gourds, pumpkins and tobacco are all native Indian crops!

Federal Recognition

The United States government's official acknowledgement of a group of Indians as a tribe that is eligible for government benefits, programs and funds.

Footwear

South Dakota Indians wore different footwear depending on their tribe and environment. Moccasins were made mostly of animal skin. Sandals were made of rawhide or plant material.

First on the Land

Prehistoric peoples lived along the Missouri River in South Dakota until around the 13th century, possibly forced out by drought. The Arikara or Ree Indians then migrated here, as did the Hidatsa and Mandan. During the 1600s and 1700s other tribes were pushed west by enemy tribes or pioneers.

G is for . . .

Games

Adults played ball and other games of chance or skill. Indian children spun tops, fought pretend battles, did target-shooting, walked on stilts, played hide and seek, or competed to see who could hold their breath the longest!

Go To These Exciting Indian Events in Our State!:

Sinte Gleska Annual Founders' Day Celebration Traditional and Contest Wacipi – January, Mission; Annual Wacipi at S.D. State University – February, Brookings; Sisseton Wahpeton Oyate Annual Wacipi – July, Agency Village; Flandreau Santee Pow Wow – July, Flandreau; West Bend Annual Pow Wow – July, West Bend; Annual Yankton Sioux Tribe Pow Wow – August, Lake Andes; Crow Creek Sioux Wacipi – August, Ft. Thompson; Kul-Wicasa Oyate Fair & Wacipi – August, Lower Brule; Annual Rosebud Fair and Wacipi Rodeo – August, Rosebud; Annual Cheyenne River Sioux Tribe Labor Day Fair & Rodeo Celebration – August, Cheyenne-Eagle Butte; Annual He Sapa Wacipi - Black Hills Pow Wow & Art Market – October, Rapid City.

Gens

Group of related members from different tribes.

Gathering

Native Americans gathered natural materials for food, fuel, baskets, clothing, and housing. American Indians tribes also hunted to meet basic needs. Even though some tribes planted crops, most did some kind of gathering.

Gorgets

Beautiful ornaments hung around the neck or from ears; their significance, if any, is unknown.

Gourds

Hollowed-out shell of a gourd plant's dried fruit which often grew into a specific shape. Indians raised many species of gourds. They were used for spoons, bowls, masks, rattles, and even storage.

Gall

Born in South Dakota in 1840. Hunkpapa Sioux chief who was Sitting Bull's adopted younger brother and military strategist. Played a key role at Little Big Horn. He returned to North Dakota from Canada five years later, settling at the Standing Rock Reservation. There, he began to accept white ways. He even traveled to Washington D.C. with a Lakota delegation.

H is for . . .

Hatchet

A small, short-handled ax, primarily used as a tool, not as a weapon. When settlers moved in, stone hatchets were replaced with iron ones.

Hair

Indians used hair as a textile. Hair from bison, mountain sheep, elk, moose, deer, dog, rabbit, beaver, or even humans were used to weave cloth, make wigs, or stuff pillows, balls, dolls or drumsticks.

Horn and Hooves

Indians used animal horn to make spoons and dishes. Hooves were made into rattles and bird beaks were used for decoration.

Hear the Message

The Ghost Dance Religion spread among the Plains Tribes in the late 1880s. It centered around returning to native ways and living together in harmony. It preached that the earth would soon die, to come alive again for only the Indians. The religion called for ridding oneself of the white ways, prayer, meditation, chanting and dancing – particularly the Ghost Dance. Although the founder of the religion was Paiute, many Plains tribes practiced this religion, including the Sioux. The spread and popularity of this new religion was the cause of the Massacre at Wounded Knee.

Heroes

One of the most well known warrior societies was the Kioa's Kiotsenko, also called the Principal Dogs and the Ten Bravest. It was an exclusive society, limited to 10 warriors who had proven themselves repeatedly. Their leader wore a long sash that dropped to the ground. In battle it was speared to the earth and the leader fought from that spot, only moving when another Principal Dog released the sash.

Hunters

Early Indian peoples were hunters who used wooden spears with stone points to kill many kinds of large mammals that are extinct today, such as mammoths and mastodons!

Horses

Spaniards brought the horse to America. At first, Indians were afraid of the horse or thought it was sacred. Later, Indians "broke" horses gently, often "hypnotizing" them with a blanket. Horses were used for transportation, trade, barter or payment. Some Indians ate horse meat in hopes of gaining the animal's power.

Historic Hills

Around A.D. 500, Mound Builders began to settle east of the Missouri River along the Big Sioux River and Big Stone Lake. They built more than 100 dome-shaped earthen mounds used as burial chambers. Near Brandon there once stood 38 mounds, known as the Eminija Mounds. These people vanished after A.D. 1000, probably from a disease epidemic.

I is for . . .

Indian Removal Act of 1830

This federal act gave President Andrew Jackson the power to relocate tribes east of the Mississippi to an "Indian Territory." The forced removal of the southeast Indians later became known as the "Trail of Tears."

Indian Scout

This term for a guide applied to Indians or white-skinned people who served that role.

Indian Reservation

A tract of land set aside by a government for Indians to live on.

Indian Wars

The Sioux were the most famous of the Plains Indian warriors. An ongoing group of raids, counterraids, skirmishes and military action lasting from the 1850s to the 1890s is known as the Sioux Wars. The phases of them were: the Grattan Affair, Little Crow's War (also known as the Minnesota Uprising), the War for the Bozeman Trail (also known as Red Cloud's War), the War for the Black Hills (also known as Sitting Bull's and Crazy Horse's War), and the Massacre at Wounded Knee.

Independence

Native American tribes are sovereign nations. That means they are independent. Some even issue their own passports! However, Native Americans are also considered citizens of the United States and enjoy all the rights and privileges of U.S. citizens.

Indian

In 1493, Christopher Columbus called the native people he met in North America "Indians" because he mistakenly believed he had sailed to India! Today, this term includes the aborigines of North and South America.

Indian Ladder

Indians made ladders by trimming branches off a tree. Some were left at consistent intervals to provide steps.

Indian Tribes in South Dakota

At one time or another, these tribes have lived in the state of South Dakota:

Cheyenne, Kiowa, Mandan, Omaha, Ponca, Sioux, Winnebago

J is for . . .

Just So You Know . . .

Today you can find many South Dakota Indians that follow some traditional ways. But there are also many who are entrepreneurs, doctors, lawyers, educators and even politicians! If you visit a reservation or cultural event, make sure you know visitor etiquette. Often dances are religious ceremonies and should be observed as such; religious dances should not be applauded. Photography, videotaping and drawing are all important issues - check with the tribe or individual before any is started.

Jesuits

Roman Catholic priests called Jesuits were among the first to meet and live with the North American Indians. Their writings, sent back to Europe, serve as one of today's best references to early Indian life.

Justice?

For hundreds of years, Native Americans have not received justice from federal and state governments. Native Americans have had nearly all their land taken away. Native Americans still have to fight for their rights in courts across the land.

Judicial Termination

Modern term to describe current efforts by various U.S. government agencies and officials (especially the judicial system) to legally decrease the sovereignty of independent Indian tribes.

Just In Time!

The Indian Arts and Crafts Act of 1990 makes it against the law to pretend that an item has been made by Native Americans if it is really not. It is illegal to offer or display for sale, or sell any art or craft product in a way that falsely suggests it is Indian produced.

Jerked Meat

Thin strips of buffalo, elk, deer or other animal meat which is dried on racks in the sun; also called "jerky."

K is for . . .

Kiowa

Migrated to the Black Hills area of western South Dakota after getting permission from the Crow, in the early 1700s. The tribe began to acquire Plains Indians traits here. Migrated away from South Dakota in the late 1700s.

Kill Site

An archaeological site where remains of many animals have been found along with human artifacts. Many kill sites have been useful to scientists in learning how ancient American Indians lived.

Killed Pottery

Pottery placed in a grave as an offering to the dead person was called killed pottery. A hole was formed in its base during creation. Often broken pottery was placed in a grave because Indians believed the spirit of the dead person would then be released and could travel.

Knife

Made from various materials such as bone, reed, stone, wood, antler, shell, metal, or animal teeth (bear, beaver, etc.), knives were used as weapons but also creative handiwork.

Knowledge

Knowledge is power. Native Americans shared knowledge with the first European settlers. Native Americans showed settlers how to plant crops, which plants were safe to eat, and other knowledge about the land.

Knots

Tied on bowstrings, spearhead and arrowhead lashings, snowshoes, and other items, knots were sometimes used to keep track of the days like a calendar—each knot equaled 1 day.

L is for . . .

Linguistic Families

There are 56 related groups of American Indian languages. A few of these speech families include Iroquoian, Algonquian, Siouan, Muskogean, Athapascan, and Wakashan.

Leggings

Both men and women wore cloth or skin covering, which were often decorated with quills, beads, or painted designs, for their legs.

Lost Tribes of Israel

This historic theory has been floating around since 721 BC. The 10 lost tribes of Israel are supposedly groups of people gathered together by Sargon, the King of Assyria. Some say he cast out 10 of the 12 tribes of Israel. Many have tried to prove that the American Indians are these missing tribes!

Lake Francis Case

Excavations here at the Crow Creek Village site overlooking this lake have uncovered the remains of a prehistoric farming village. What is thought to be the largest ancient massacre site was found here, dating from the early 1300s.

Lodge

The term for a type of Indian house that was usually a permanent dwelling. The population of a tribe was often estimated by its number of lodges.

Land Loss

Native Americans lost their land in many ways. Conflicts with other tribes, colonization, European settlement, treaties, and removal took away Indian lands.

Lance

Spear used for hunting and war. The hunting lance had a short shaft and a broad, heavy head. The war lance was light and had a long shaft.

Laramie Treaty

Signed by the Teton Sioux and Arapaho in 1868. Gave them 22 million acres plus daily food, farm animals and equipment plus the assistance of teachers, doctors and blacksmiths. But soon, the whites broke the treaty by going onto reservation land, sold the promised food to others and left the Indians so angry that they fought back for their rights.

Lariat

These throw ropes made of rawhide, buffalo hair, or horsehair sometimes measured up to 20 feet long!

M is for . . .

Maize

Also called Indian Corn. Known as a "cereal" plant because it probably began as some form of grass. The Indians in our state figured out every possible way to use corn as a food. The only thing the white man added was the creation of "corn flakes!"

Mitchell Prehistoric Indian Village

Occupied by farmer-hunters around 1,000 years ago. About 1,000 people may have lived in 70 timber-frame mud-plastered lodges. They hunted buffalo, foraged for small game and wild plants and grew corn, beans, squash, tobacco and sunflowers. Now a National Historic Landmark.

Mortar and Pestle

A two-part milling tool, with a bowl-shaped stone, plus a club-shaped stone (or wooden bowl and wooden club), used for pulverizing or grinding plants or animal matter.

Medicine

Medicine could be good or bad. Medicines or charms were placed in a bag by young warriors and carried at all times. Some of the roots, leaves and bark that Indians in our state used as medicine are being rediscovered and used by today's doctors!

Moccasins

Indian shoes made of animal skin.

Medicine Man

A person who got the power to heal the sick through a secret means, usually from a dream or visions.

Mandan

Once lived along the moth of the White River in South Dakota. Often painted by famous Indian artist George Catlin. Explorers Lewis and Clark and famous Shoshone Indian guide, Sacagawea, spent time with the tribe. Known for their extremely large earth-lodges that as many as 60 people lived in. The lodges had wood frames and were so strong many Indians could be on their tops at once. They used the roofs to play games, gossip, store possessions or "hang out."

N is for . . .

Nomadic

A way of life in which people frequently moved from one location to another in search of food. "Seminomadic" people had permanent villages, but left them in certain seasons to hunt, fish, or gather wild plant foods.

New Life Lodge

This sacred Cheyenne ceremony was a version of the Sun Dance. Performed annually to renew the Indians' world. It was an 8-day ceremony. During it, the Indians built a special lodge with a sacred pole. Rituals were performed by medicine men, and there was also much dancing and even self-torture before the pole. Banned by the federal government in 1910.

Nation

There are many Indian nations located within the United States, such as the Sioux Nation. Indian nations are called nations because their governments and laws are independent of and separate from the U.S. government. The federal government must have "government to government" relations with these Indian nations, just as it would with foreign nations, like England or Spain.

November

In 1990, President George Bush approved a joint resolution designating November 1990 "National American Indian Heritage Month." Similar proclamations have been issued each year since 1994.

Names

Indian names were often changed during one's lifetime. These names could be derived from events that happened during the person's birth, childhood, adolescence, war service, or retirement from active tribal life. Some names came from dreams, some were inherited, and sometimes names were stolen or taken in revenge. Today some Indians maintain old, traditional Indian names, while others take modern names. Since settlers often did not read or write Indian languages, they recorded Indian names phonetically (as they "sounded"). Thus Indian names were often misspelled.

Nakota

The Sioux Yankton and Yanktonai branches use this name for themselves. The Yankton Nakota lived along the Missouri River in southeast South Dakota. The Yanktonai lived north of them in eastern South Dakota. The two branches together are sometimes called the Middle Sioux.

National Museum of the American Indian

The Smithsonian's National Museum of the American Indian on the National Mall in Washington, D.C., symbolizes a deeper understanding between America's first citizens and those who have come to make these shores their home.

O is for . . .

Old Bones

No one knows for sure when the first people came to North America, but scientists have dated bones and artifacts discovered at Clovis, New Mexico around 11,200 years old. Testing on a skeleton found on the Channel Islands, off the coast of California showed they were about 13,000 years old. And, evidence of human habitation in southern New Mexico suggests that people may have been there as far back as 38,000 years ago.

Oahe Lake

Named for an Indian mission; word is Siouan for "a safe place on which to stand."

Origins

Some scientists believe that Native Americans actually came across a land bridge between Asia and North America. They say that during an ice age thousands of years ago, the water level was much lower and people could have walked between the two continents.

Omaha

Bands of this tribe had villages in South Dakota at one time. Lived in permanent villages between the Platte, Niobrara and Missouri rivers. Built large earth-lodges and cultivated crops. Carried the portable tepee with them when they went buffalo hunting. Known for their complex social structure.

Oil

Indians extracted oil from the many layers of fat that came with fresh bear meat. The fat was boiled down in earthen pots to produce the oil, which was stored in gourds and pots. The oil was used for cooking and even beautifying the body! Indians would mix red pigment with the oil, add the fragrances of cinnamon and sassafras, and rub it all over their bodies.

Orators

Many Indian leaders were excellent public speakers. Powerful and dramatic speakers were vital to leaders who wanted to influence their tribe. Watch for famous Indian quotations in literature and textbooks!

Office of Indian Education Programs

This is a service organization devoted to providing quality education opportunities for American Indian people. Established in the latter part of the nineteenth century to carry out the federal government's education commitment to Indian tribes, it has become the only national education system for American Indian children and adults.

P is for . . .

Powwow

The original form of the word meant "medicine man." Medicine men would often use noise motion and confusion to scare away harmful spirits and cure people. It was also a gathering to talk about political matters. Today, the powwow is an event where Indians gather to sing, perform ceremonial dances, and share cultural pride and traditions.

Pine Ridge Reservation

Home to the Oglala Sioux. Largest of all the Sioux reservations, with 1.7 million acres. Established in 1889. Second largest reservation in the nation. Wounded Knee Creek, site of the Massacre at Wounded Knee, is on this reservation.

Ponca

This tribe could be found in South Dakota along the banks of the Niobrara River. Lived in villages, farmed, hunted and fished. Removed from their homelands in 1876, and involved in a famous precedent-setting court case in 1879.

Paint

Indians used many natural materials to make paint, like clay mixed with oil or grease. Yellow "paint" was made with the gall bladder of a buffalo! Why did they paint their faces or bodies? Indians used paint to look scary or beautiful, to disguise themselves, or to protect their skin from sunburn or insect bites. Indians often applied red paint because it symbolized strength and success. That is why settlers often referred to the Indians as Red Men.

Paha Sapa

What the Indians call the Black Hills.

Pemmican

Indian food made of animal meat, which was dried in the sun, pounded together with fat and berries. The mixture was packed into skin bags and used primarily while on the trail.

Papoose

An American Indian infant aged between birth and one year is called a papoose. This word also refers to the way infants were bundled and carried by its mother. A papoose spent most of his or her days snugly wrapped in a kind of cradle made of skins or bark and a wooden frame that hung on the mother's back. This sturdy frame also allowed a mother to lean her papoose against a tree or rock within sight as she worked.

Pottery

Indian pottery was made from built-up spirals of clay that were molded or paddled, or a combination of the two methods. Most pottery served as cooking vessels.

Picture History

Some Indians kept a record of time and important events by painting or drawing pictures or symbols on skin, bark, or stone.

Q is for . . .

Quillwork

Indians used the quills of porcupine or birds to make a type of embroidery. Quills were dyed with juice from berries and other materials. When they were ready to be used, the quills were either mashed with teeth or softened with hot water and flattened with rocks. The quills were then laced into moccasins, shirts, pipe covers, and other items. Beads which Indians received by trading with settlers eventually replaced quillwork.

Quality

Native American arts and crafts are known for their excellent craftsmanship and striking designs. This work is often influenced by things found in nature especially plants and animals.

Quiver

Case used to hold arrows; made of woven plant materials or animal skins.

Quarry Site

A location where Indians went for workable stone such as flint and made stone tools.

Quirt

A short riding whip with a wood, bone, or horn handle.

R is for . . .

Rain Dancing

The rain dance ceremony, performed to encourage rainfall, was common among Indian religions because good weather is vital for a successful harvest. Rainmakers were in tune with nature; there are actual reported cases of Indians producing or preventing rain!

Roots

Indians used plant roots for food, medicine, dye, baskets, cloth, rope, salt, flavoring, and just to chew!

Rattles

Indians of South Dakota made rattles from bird beaks, animal hooves, bones, pods, seashells, turtle shells and other animal parts. The rattles are used in ceremonies.

Red Cloud

Famous Oglala Sioux chief. Born about 1822. In 1865, he and 2,000 warriors began the fight to save the tribe's hunting grounds. He wanted a treaty with the U.S. that promised no more forts would be built along the Bozeman Trail. He and his warriors succeeded many times, finally getting the government to agree. The resulting treaty was the 1868 Ft. Laramie Treaty. Red Cloud later met the president and visited New York City. The Red Cloud Agency (reservation) was moved to South Dakota after Little Big Horn, and renamed Pine Ridge. Red Cloud was known for trying to keep peace with the whites. Counted 80 coups in his lifetime. Died in 1909.

Rawhide

Untanned animal hide. The "green" hide was stretched on the ground or over a frame. Flesh and fat were removed. The skin was dried, washed, then buried with wood ashes which made the hair come off. Used by the South Dakota Indian to make drumheads, lash lodge poles, mend broken objects and in many other ways.

Reservations

The U.S. government set aside, or "reserved," land for the Indians. These reservations originally served as a sort of prison during the beginning stages of Indian removal. At that time, reservations provided the government with some control over Indian activity and residency. This land was usually considerably less desirable land than the Indians' native territories. Today's reservations are lands that are tribally held, yet protected by the government.

Removal

The U.S. government policy of the 1830s-1850s that removed Indians from their native lands to new lands, primarily west of the Mississippi River.

S is for . . .

Sioux

This tribe is made up of different groups with varying histories and customs. The Sioux are collectively known as the Dakota. There are four ancestral branches of the Sioux, each containing different bands. South Dakota is the heartland of this once mighty Indian tribe. The Teton Lakota, Yankton Nakota, and the Yanktonai Nakota all were divisions of the Sioux in South Dakota. Their 30,000 members make it one of the largest tribal groups in America today. Came here around 1750, after being forced westward by other tribes.

Sacred Bundles

A group of objects treasured by a tribe. They were well-guarded and often taken into battle. The items were publicly shown only on very important occasions.

Shield

A piece of "armor" made of a rawhide-covered frame, which was carried into battle. Shields also could be decorative and religious objects. Many tribes make shields today as an art form!

Sweatlodge

Structure used for ritual purification by sweating from exposure to very hot fires or hot steam from pouring water over hot stones. Also called a sweathouse, for some tribes also doubling as clubhouses.

Shaman

Medicine man and spiritual leader who was supposed to have special healing power from another world.

Spotted Tail

Brulé Sioux who won his wife at age 19 in a knife duel. He rose in the ranks and became chief by surrendering himself to spare his people at Ft. Laramie. Counseled peace with whites. Appointed as chief of both the Lakota Sioux agencies as a reward for not having fought against the whites in South Dakota. He later arranged for Crazy Horse to surrender. He was killed in 1881 by his rival Crow Dog; he was 68 years old.

Saddle

While some Indians did use saddles on their horses, most rode bareback!

Secret Societies

Indians had secret groups, usually organized for religious or ceremonial reasons. Each society had a purpose, such as to cure disease.

Sitting Bull

Famous Sioux warrior, tribal chief of the Hunkpapa Sioux and leader of the allied tribes in the battle against Gen. Custer. Born in 1831. Went on his first buffalo hunt about the age of 10; counted his first coup at age 14. Later became a medicine man. Even though he and the other Sioux chiefs won the battle at the Little Big Horn, he was forced to flee into Canada. Later came back and surrendered at Ft. Buford. Held prisoner for a while, then allowed to settle on Standing Rock Reservation. In 1890, he invited his nephew, Kicking Bear, to the reservation to demonstrate the Ghost Dance. The worried Indian Agent ordered the arrest of Sitting Bull, and in the chaos between the dancers and the military, Sitting Bull was killed.

T is for . . .

Tobacco

A sacred plant early Indians used to make offering to their gods, cure diseases, bring good luck, seal agreements and bind treaties.

Treaties

Written agreements between the U. S. government and the Indians, most of which involved the Indians giving up their native lands.

Throwing Stick

A sling or grooved stick used to hurl a lance or spear. It was used by South Dakota Indians before bows and arrows.

Totem

The spirit of some natural object (usually an animal) taken by an Indian, tribe or family to guard over them.

Teton

The largest branch of the Sioux tribe. Contains the Oglala, Brulé, Hunkpapa, Miniconjou, Oohenonpa, Itazipco, and Sihasapa bands. Lived in the Black Hills area of South Dakota. Sometimes called the Western Sioux. The name they use for themselves is Lakota.

Tomahawk

A club, axe or hammer used to chop wood, drive stakes in the ground or as a weapon.

Tracking

To follow a trail by finding a sign such as a broken blade of grass, a moved stone or moccasin track. Indians learned to trail as children, so that they could find food, track enemies and disguise their own signs.

Teeth

South Dakota Indians hung teeth on cords to make necklaces.

Tribe

A group of Indians with shared culture, history, original territory, ancestry, social organization, and governmental structure. A tribe may contain several bands of Indians.

Thunderbird

A mythological Indian figure, as well as a part of the constellations for many Indians. Thunderbird mythology is mostly different from tribe to tribe, in general either coexisting with ancestors as an actual bird, or appearing as a spiritual nature god. The Thunderbird was good to the people in either case. Much mythology ties the thunderbird with thunder, lightning and storms.

Taimay

The Kiowa worshipped this stone image. This trait is typical of ancient Mexican and Central American Indians. Along with the different language they speak, their worship of the taimay suggests they may have an ancient connection with these very different people.

U is for . . .

U.S. Bureau of Indian Affairs

Provides public services such as law enforcement, land records, economic development, and education to Indians. Known for mismanagement and ethical problems.

U.S. Army

Many Native Americans have fought bravely for the United States Army. Many have also given their lives for a country that was not always accepting of them.

Unique

Each and every tribe has its own unique customs, language, and traditions.

U.S. Indian Schools

The Bureau of Indian Affairs operates hundreds of federal schools around the nation. Enrollment of Native American children measures in the thousands!

U.S. Indian Reorganization Act

Passed by Congress in 1934, the act authorized Indian tribes to establish and conduct their own governments, and to form businesses.

U.S. President

Once called Great White Father by Indians.

U.S. Colonists

Called Long Knives or Big Knives by early Indians, who also called English explorers "Coat Men."

U.S. Indian Wars

The U.S. War Department has compiled an official list of "Indian Wars" that occurred in the United States. Over 50 wars were fought between the U.S. and the Indians during the period of 1790-1850.

V is for . . .

Vessels

Indians carried water in special gourds shaped liked bottles, called water vessels.

Village Councils

These were held in the town (council) house and occurred to discuss and decide important matters. Harmony and agreement was essential to tribal unity. Rather than vote on issues, they were discussed until everyone was satisfied. Anyone who wanted to could speak freely. Everyone did not always agree on the outcome, but everyone avoided conflict by pushing their case.

Vegetable Dyes

Indians could not buy color from the store like we can today. Instead, they created many different colors from the things they found on earth like plants, flowers, shrubs, trees, roots, and berries. They made beautiful and unique reds, oranges, yellows, greens, browns, and violets. These dyes were used for baskets, pottery, weaving, body makeup, and clothing.

Very Hungry

There were Indians who here hunters, gatherers and foragers, that often ate whatever they could find! How hungry would you have to be to eat what they sometimes ate: reptiles, larvae, and insects?

Villages

Many South Dakota Indians lived in villages! Villages were formed around different clans or bands within the tribe, but could also contain different clans living together. Villages were usually permanent settlements, although semi-nomadic tribes have been known to migrate between permanent villages.

Vermillion

Founded in 1859 following a treaty with the Yankton Sioux, who later traded at the post here.

W is for . . .

War Bonnet

Special headdress worn into battle, often adorned with feathers.

War Pony

Horse, often painted with colorful paint and ridden into battle.

Women

Indian women in some South Dakota tribes were poor and hardworking, like the men. But in some tribes, women had many rights, including becoming chief!

Wounded Knee

Site of the December 29, 1890 unnecessary massacre of Indian men, women and children. At the time, a large Ghost Dance was planned on the Pine Ridge Reservation. Big Foot's band was traveling to the reservation, not to participate, but to join Red Cloud's band. Intercepted by the Army, the band was ordered to set up camp at Wounded Knee Creek. Here, a skirmish broke out then suddenly evolved into a full-fledged attack by the Army's heavy artillery placed around the camp. The result was at least 150 Indian men, women and children killed. This marked the end of the Indian Wars on the Great Plains. Later, in 1973, a 71-day American Indian Movement occupation at the same site resulted in the killing of two Indians by federal agents, and is called the Siege at Wounded Knee.

War Dance

Indian braves danced this before going into battle. The dance was a way of assembling the braves and getting them to commit to the fight ahead.

Whistle

Indians from South Dakota made them from the wing bones of birds. The whistles made the sound of the bird the bones came from! Used to communicate, signal, sound an alarm or even flirt with a maiden!

White Man

Indians generally called them Pale Face, a name the white men themselves suggested!

War Club

A weapon made of stone, bone, or wood in the shape of a club.

Winnebago

This central Great Lakes woodland tribe lived in villages of rectangular bark lodges, but also went on the trail to hunt buffalo. They hunted, fished, gathered and farmed for their food. The "Winnebago Way" means to live with a reverence for nature. After the Black Hawk War, they were relocated four times. The third time brought them to South Dakota.

XYZ are for . . .

Xenophobe

A xenophobe is someone who is afraid of foreign people, their customs and cultures, or foreign things. Many of the first European settlers were afraid of Native American cultures.

You Bet!

Some Native Americans say that Casinos make a lot of money. Others say that too many people have a gambling problem. In the 1980s and 1990s, many tribes discussed whether or not gambling casinos should be allowed. Now that many casinos have been built across the country, the debate has switched to how it should be controlled.

Young-Man-Afraid-of-His-Horses

Oglala Sioux inducted into the Cheyenne Crooked Lances warrior society. Later settled on the Pine Ridge Reservation. His father was Man-Afraid-Of-His-Horses, an incorrect translation of his native name Tasunkakokipap. His native name actually meant "he that is so powerful the sight of his horses inspires fear."

ZZZZZZ...

Shamans and medicine men were not the only people who had access to the spirit world. Indians believed that people could make contact with spirits every night in their dreams! Dreamers could travel back to the time of man's creation or far ahead into their own futures. They also believed that dreams contained warnings or commands from the spirits. Many tribes felt that they had to act out their dreams as soon as they awoke. If an Indian dreamed about bathing, for example, he would run to his neighbors' houses first thing in the morning, and his neighbors would throw kettles full of cold water over him.

Y... Or, "Why?"

1. Why do you think Indian warriors carried charms with them? Some Indian medicines have been scientifically proven to have true healing power and are still used today. Do you think their charms had any real power to help them win battles?
2. Why do you think the American government kept relocating Indians onto reservations and then making the reservations smaller and smaller?
3. Why did Indians use items such as a pipe in ceremonies? What kinds of symbolic objects do we use in ceremonies today?
4. Why and how did Indians use natural materials in creative ways?
5. Many Indian tribes are running successful businesses on their reservations today. There is one industry that many tribes are making a lot of money at. Do you know what this is? Hint: "I'll bet you do!"

Which Famous Native American Am I?

Solve the puzzle!

Word Bank

Black Elk	Crazy Horse	Sitting Bull	Sequoia
Sacajawea	Chief Joseph	Geronimo	Pocahontas

Down

1. This Shoshone woman joined Lewis and Clark as their guide and translator and helped make the expedition a success! Hint: She has 4 "a"s in her name!
4. This man gave the Cherokee their first alphabet so that they could write. Until then, they communicated only by speaking and drawing pictures. Hint: A famous ancient tree also has the same name!
5. He was one of the fiercest of Indian warriors! He fought against white settlers in Arizona and New Mexico to keep his people from being pushed off their lands. Hint: Jump!

Across

2. A legend says that this brave Algonquian woman saved the life of Englishman John Smith. Hint: Disney produced a movie about her.
3. He fought at Little Bighorn when he was only 13! He was also a wise "shaman" who saw visions and could advise people. Hint: Part of his name is an animal with antlers!
6. He was a great Sioux warrior who won the battle against General Custer at Little Bighorn in 1876. Hint: His horse was not crazy!
7. A leader of the Lakota (Sioux) tribe who lived on the Standing Rock Reservation in North Dakota after the battle of Little Bighorn. He tried to make conditions better for his people there, so the U.S. government called him a "troublemaker." Hint: He did not sit all the time!
8. A wise and brave chief of the Nez Percé who tried to bring his people to Canada to escape war. He said, "From where the sun now stands, I will fight no more forever." Hint: His father's name was "Old Joseph."

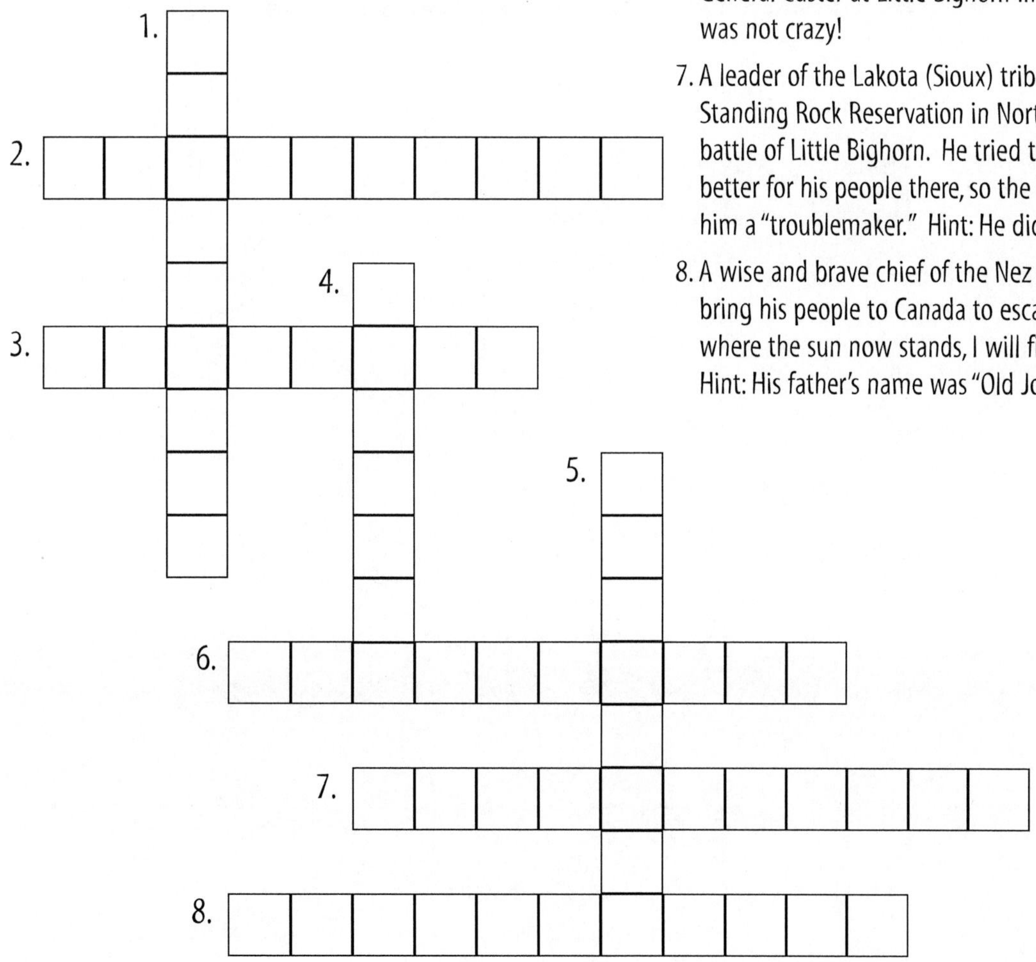

Answer Key: 1. Sacajawea; 2. Pocahontas; 3. Black Elk; 4. Sequoia; 5. Geronimo; 6. Crazy Horse; 7. Sitting Bull; 8. Chief Joseph

Different Ways for Different Indians!

North American Indian tribes are divided into different areas. In each of these areas, tribes shared common ways of living with each other. They might make similar arts or crafts, they might eat the same foods, or they might have had the same beliefs. These activities are all part of their "culture." Each area had its own culture, which was different from the tribes in all the other areas.

Below is a map of all the different groups of Indian tribes in North America. Color each area with a different color. You will see a colorful picture of how Native Americans can all be called "Indians" but still have very different cultures!

Celebration!

Powwows are big festivals where Native Americans gather to sing, dance, and eat together. It is a time to celebrate and show pride in their culture. Powwows can last from one afternoon to several days. The Indians dress in native costumes and dance ancient dances to the beating of drums.

Artists sell their arts and crafts. You might be able to buy some real Native American food cooked on an open fire. Native Americans go to powwows to be with each other, share ideas, and just have fun! Most powwows are also open to people who are not Indian. It's a great place to learn about Native American culture!

If you went to a powwow this weekend, what do you think you would see? What do you think might NOT be there? Circle the objects you think you would see at a powwow. Put an X through those you probably won't see.

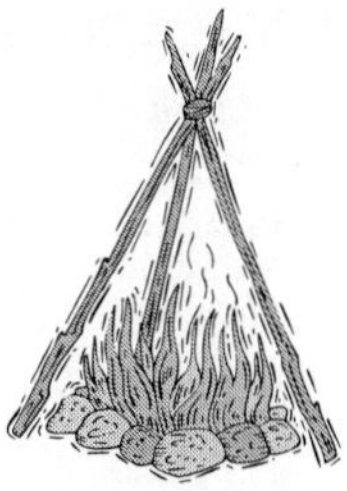

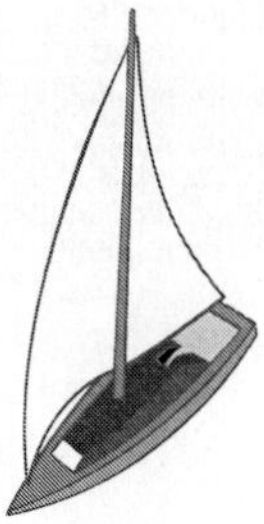

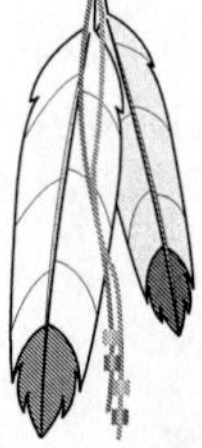

Answer Key: Circled objects are: beads, moccasins, open fire, drums, feathers, baskets, kids, food, drums, horse.

Make an Indian Weaving!

Many Native Americans used weaving to create useful things like sashes (belts), bags, mats, and blankets. They used animal hair to make yarn, and dyed the yarn with natural dyes from fruits and other plants. They also used some plant fibers, like cotton, to make weaving thread.

Weave a small Native American mat of your own. Use different colors of yarn to create a beautiful pattern in your weaving. Place a favorite object on the mat or hang it on your wall!

Prepare the "loom"

Cut a piece of cardboard 5 inches wide and 6 inches long. Along the two 5-inch sides (the "short" sides), have an adult cut slits 1/4 inch deep. These slits should be 1/2 inch apart from each other. So, on each short side you will have 9 slits.

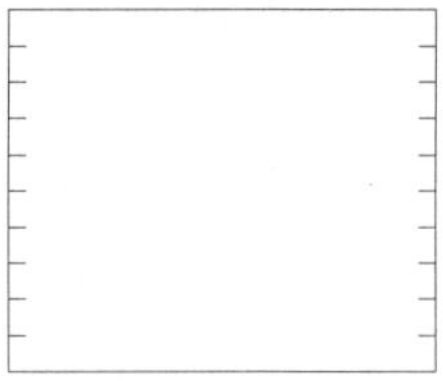

Directions:

1. Take a long piece of yarn and bring it from the back through the first slit (the one next to the edge of the cardboard.) The end of the yarn will hang down behind the cardboard.

2. Bring the yarn right across the front of the cardboard to the slit opposite the one your yarn came through.

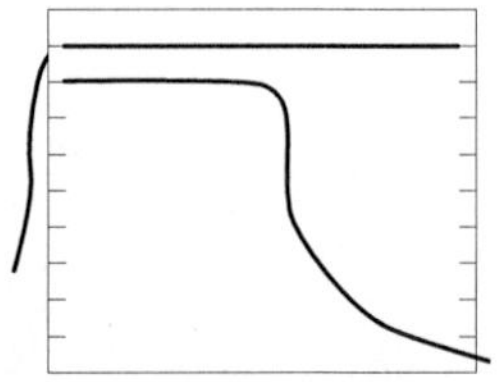

3. Now bring the yarn under the back of the cardboard and then up again through the second slit.

4. Repeat #2 and #3, until you have 9 strands of yarn across the front of your cardboard!

5. Then cut the yarn and tie the two loose ends in the back of the cardboard.

6. Take another piece of yarn and start feeding it through the 9 strands, going over one, under the next over the next, etc. When you get to the end, pull the yarn behind the cardboard and around to the front, and begin again. This time, whatever strand you went over, go under. And whatever strand you went under, go over.

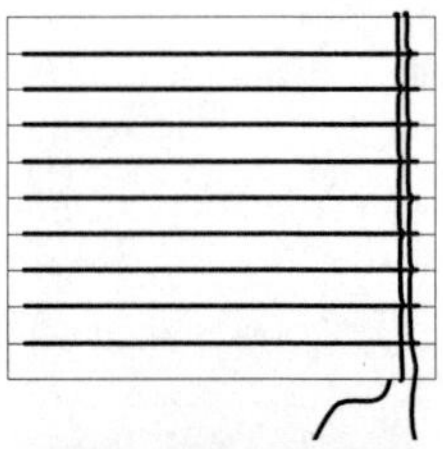

7. Repeat this pattern until the front of your cardboard in covered. Then cut the yarn in the back of the cardboard, and trim it to create a fringe for your mat!

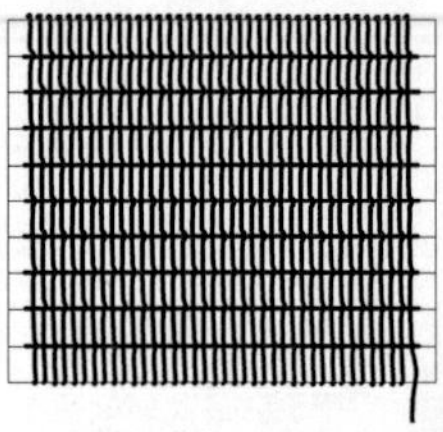

Tips:

- For a wild look, use variegated or different colored yarn!
- For a tighter mat, push the under/over strands up against the previous strands during weaving.
- To keep your mat from unravelling, tie neighboring fringe together up close to the mat.

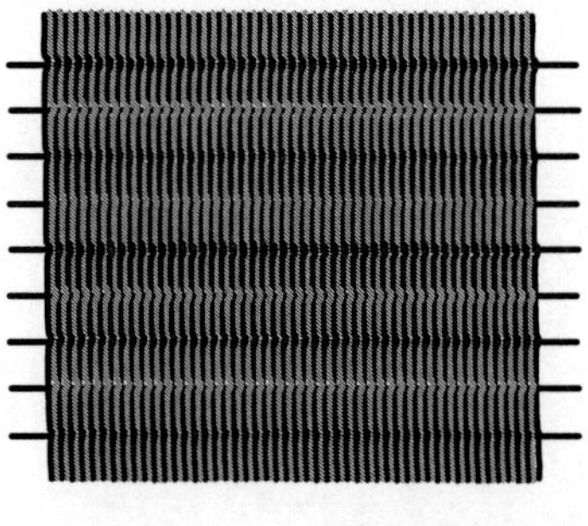

Finders Keepers?

Native Americans have many buried treasures. For hundreds of years, special objects would sometimes be buried with Native Americans, or maybe they would just be lost. Archeologists used to dig for interesting artifacts in old Native American gravesites. They would keep the Native American bones or the arrowheads, rattles, masks and other objects that they found. But this made the Native Americans feel like they were being robbed.

In 1990, the U.S. government passed a law that said that no one could look for or take these Native American objects anymore. And whoever had any already had to give them back to the people they belonged to. This is called repatriation

Help the archeologist return the artifact to a Native American.

Fast Fact

An artifact is an object that was made by people a long time ago for some useful purpose.

Busy Hands!

Before modern times, Native Americans didn't have stores where they went to buy things. They made everything they needed.

What did Indians make with their own hands? Use the Word Bank and pictures to find out!

Word Bank

blanket	moccasins	arrows	pottery	canoe
mat	food	jewelry	pouch	box

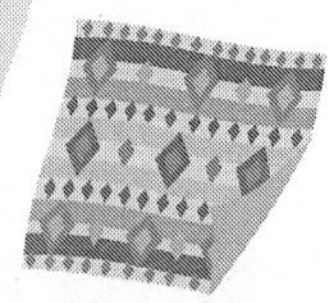 ___ ___ ___

 ___ ___ ___ ___

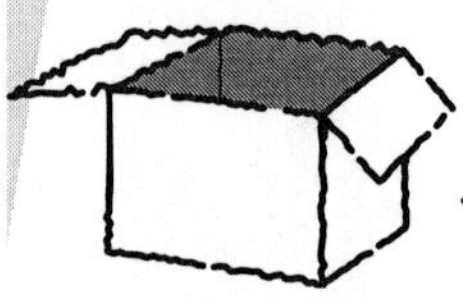 ___ ___ ___

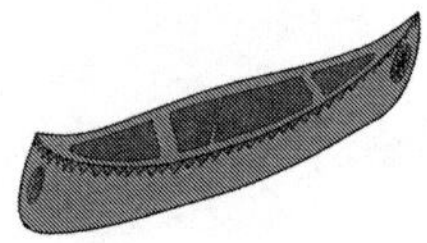 ___ ___ ___ ___ ___

 ___ ___ ___ ___ ___ ___ ___

 ___ ___ ___ ___ ___

 ___ ___ ___ ___ ___ ___ ___ ___ ___ ___

 ___ ___ ___ ___ ___ ___

 ___ ___ ___ ___ ___ ___ ___

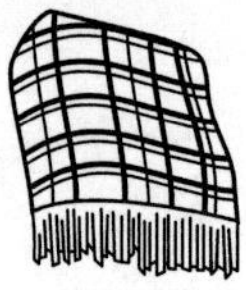 ___ ___ ___ ___ ___ ___ ___

American Indians Today

Beginning with the first letter of each group of letters, cross out every other letter to discover some new words. You may not have heard of these before, but you can read all about them!

1. Many Indians live on these, but many more do not!

TRYELSDEBRNVJAOTPIPOWNASX

____

2. Many Indians have been poor for a long time because for many years the government took away their lands and their ability to make a living.

TPKOOVWEBRNTXYA

____

3. Many Indians have been studying hard at school and going to college in order to earn more money. Education helps the Indians make their lives better. These Native Americans are working to become:

TSJUMCBCFEYSMSOFPUVL

____

4. This is a big term that means Native Americans have worked hard to get the U.S. government to let them rule themselves. This means that they have their own laws and make their own decisions. They are like a separate country inside the U.S.! Now, try and see if you can get your parents to give you the same thing!

TSGENLBF ***JDGEETSEWRAMCIHNUAKTYIKOTNU***

______________ ______________________________

Fast Fact

What do Indians work as today?

- doctors
- nurses
- factory workers
- artists
- lawyers
- actors

The same kinds of jobs any American might work at!

Native Americans Move to the City!

Solve the code to discover the mystery words!

A	B	C	D	E	F	G	H	I	J	K	L	M
✹	❀	✣	♣	➳	♥	❢	✲	✄	✆	☛	✈	✉
N	**O**	**P**	**Q**	**R**	**S**	**T**	**U**	**V**	**W**	**X**	**Y**	**Z**
✿	☆	✦	✡	✎	❦	☎	➫	✚	✖	✍	✠	✓

1. During the 1950s and 1960s, the American government paid Indians to leave their homes on reservations and move to cities to get jobs. If cities are sometimes called urban areas, then these brave Indians were called:

___ ___ ___ ___ ___   ___ ___ ___ ___ ___ ___ ___

➫ ✎ ❀ ✹ ✿   ✄ ✿ ♣ ✄ ✹ ✿ ❦

2. Many Indians chose to stay on their reservations and not move to the city. They thought that if they moved to the city, they would lose the way of life that their parents and ancestors had taught. These Indians called themselves:

___ ___ ___ ___ ___ ___ ___ ___ ___ ___ ___   ___ ___ ___ ___ ___ ___ ___

✎ ➳ ❦ ➳ ✎ ✚ ✹ ☎ ✄ ☆ ✿   ✄ ✿ ♣ ✄ ✹ ✿ ❦

3. Native Americans who moved to cities lived close to each other. They tried to keep their way of life as much as possible. They did not want to forget their religion, native art, or music. They did not want to lose their:

___ ___ ___ ___ ___ ___ ___

✣ ➫ ✈ ☎ ➫ ✎ ➳

4. Are you afraid of heights? Many people are. The Mohawk Indians are not! Many of them work hundreds of feet above the city to build steel frames for skyscrapers. People who do this work above the city are:

___ ___ ___ ___ ___   ___ ___ ___ ___ ___ ___ ___

❦ ☎ ➳ ➳ ✈   ✖ ☆ ✎ ☛ ➳ ✎ ❦

5. Today urban Indians and reservation Indians come together to celebrate their culture. They share ideas and stories. They dance and beat drums. They make and sell Indian jewelry. During these celebrations, Indians remember how much they have to be proud of! These big parties are called

___ ___ ___ ___ ___ ___ ___

✦ ☆ ✖ ✖ ☆ ✖ ❦